I Thought You Should Know

Letters, Lessons & Stories for Generations

EXPECTED END

E ×

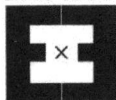

ENTERTAINMENT

ATLANTA, GA

I Thought You Should Know

Letters, Lessons & Stories for Generations

Compiled by
C. Nathaniel Brown
with
Lynn Renee Means * Necole F. Turner * Phalen Hendricks
Ellen Brown * Beatrice M. Hunter * Dezire Moore
nA' Stubbs * Nicho Charisse * Kamryn Johnson
Heaven Hightower * Sheila B.

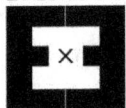

EXPECTED END

E x

ENTERTAINMENT

ATLANTA, GA

Contents

Dedication

This book is dedicated to those who desire to leave a legacy.

Acknowledgements

To everyone who supports Expected End Entertainment, you are dearly appreciated.

To Team EX3, we've come a long way but we still have a long way to go. Thank you for being on this journey with me, for changing lives for the better and providing hope and healing through what we do. It's not just what we do, it's who we are. So, I thank you.

To Team Brown, the first level of Team EX3, I love you with all my heart.

INTRODUCTION

No Holds Barred

C. Nathaniel Brown

One day, I asked my children to interview me. I told them they could ask me anything they wanted to and I would be completely honest, no hold barred. In other words, I was willing to be completely transparent about the good, the bad and the ugly of my life before them and since them.

My purpose was to share with them details about my life and what I know about my family in a way that I was never able to get from my parents. The oral traditions of African people are extraordinary. We created languages and dialects to communicate, even during slavery. We've passed down traditions and created folklore about our experiences. But we also have a history of sweeping things under the rug, keeping things that happened in our house... in our house.

As a result, we have unresolved issues, i.e. generational curses, that have been passed down from generation to generation because some things we refuse share, even though we need to know. We have unhealed wounds that continue to re-open and often get infected because of things we don't know. For example, many of us don't know our family's medical histories which could prevent us from becoming diabetic or getting cancer. Sometimes, we find out too late.

My dad said, "One day, we'll sit down and I'll give you everything you want to know so you can write a book about my life." That day hasn't arrived. Any mention of wanting to know more about his life, his feelings on certain things, or life-changing experiences become an act of futility. But I won't stop fishing because it's important to me.

My mother is a talker, the greatest storyteller I've ever know and the naturally the funniest person I've ever known. There is really is no shortage of stories she can share about herself, our family and her friends. But many of the details about all of those areas have been withheld from me for years. To her, her silence in some areas is to protect me. At least that's what she's told me over the years. Later, she also admitted that she didn't want me to look at her differently because of some things she's done that she wasn't proud of. She didn't want me to look at others differently either, like my grandmother, the closest person to perfect I've ever known. She was flawed as we all are but she never let that stop her from loving people and treating everyone like they were special... because she believed there were.

When I asked my mother to tell me about her father, she shared how she watched her mother – my grandmother – beat her father like he was a child. My mother said she never wanted me to think about or look at my grandmother differently. I didn't then and I still don't, even though she transitioned back in 1998.

My mother was practically my best friend when I was a child. I felt like I could talk to her about anything... losing my virginity, experimenting with marijuana, stealing from the corner store... Sure, I got disciplined sometimes, but she used those experiences as a teaching tool. I just didn't realize then that I needed her to be more open with me about her life and her experiences. I know some would have hurt me, but that was a risk I think we both needed to take.

So when I told me my children, no holds barred, I understood the risks on both sides. See, no holds barred means free of restrictions or hampering conventions. It's meant to convey that there are no rules or restrictions applied in a conflict or dispute. In wrestling, it refers to no restrictions on the kinds of holds that are used. In other words, there could be some things we hear or say that might sting. But some things we need to know.

You'd be surprised how much good can come from simply sharing your story. There are things that we need to know. Those we love need to know that we them. We need to hear them express it. Those we mentor need to know our experiences to learn and grow from them, to avoid the same pitfalls, and build on the things we started. Our children and grandchildren need to know family history, health history, accomplishments and failures. We have a responsibility one to another. That's why we are here. That's what this book is about. That's why I thought you should know that I love you!

C. Nathaniel Brown

Chapter 1

Dear Younger Queen

Sheila B.

My Dear and Darling Queen,

I wanted to write you, from your future me to prepare you for the path you are about to embark upon called *life*. I know it may seem like you don't have a clear path to what you are going to do or be but know this, you were born to shine. Please remember no matter what happens, know that you are a Queen, that I love you, and regardless of what you may face, you will make it. There are so many things you will see, experience and discover in your journey to me. I want you to know how incredibly special your existence is and that your internal beauty will exude light for many souls that are destined to join your journey. Never allow your circumstances and second thoughts to let you lose sight of that.

Everything in life will not be easy. How I wished I could tell you that this extended trip will be just that but I can't. I wished that I could say you will never cry, hurt, fall, fail, get angry, be wrongly accused, have regrets, feel unworthy, be embarrassed, feel scared, terrified, have your heart broken, want to run away, question your purpose, disappoint yourself/others, or make mistakes but I can't because that would be dishonest. You will indeed know all of those things and even more but never think for one moment you will not prevail because you will. I promise. It's important that you remember to have patience in all things and always practice humility, thankfulness coupled with a lot of humbleness. Even in the most difficult times of your life, always know that you are going through it for a reason. So, each time you meet a point in your life that feels weighted or dark, be sure to reflect on my words, *the moment is temporary*. You will be ok.

Be yourself. This will be the easiest thing in your life to do. You will find that a lot of people will give all their energy to be like others, to blend in with the crowd or masses. This will certainly not be you, my younger self. You will be fashionably outdated with your brown velour pants, off brand Nike sneakers and wooly mammoth coat. Also brace yourself for the carbuncles that will seem to grow overnight on your face. This may give you a slither of temptation to want to be like everyone else but just remember you are your own person. You will outgrow it all and gracefully merge into your own skin! Wait till your first high school class reunion!

Younger self, you are a talent mecca!! Dig, scrap and claw into your creative side. You will find that your ability to see art and create art will bring you joy, peace and provide you with an escape, an outlet to put your mind at ease, peace in those moments when nothing externally can do so. Poetry will liberate your mind, guide you in your writings and music will give you an entry to expressing your own melodies. Create often.

Time will teach you a number of lessons. From each one you will be able to use them to empower and inspire many. While the subjects may be harsh, you will learn to accept yourself, love yourself and define your identity. You will be tempted to hush those lessons that cause you pain, that seem to encrypt your story. You will discover that deeply embedded in you is that of a survivor. God will hear you. Be sure to speak to Him often, a lot and trust His ability to calm your storm. I wish that I could carry you through the times I know you will face; I can't. Remember, I'm speaking from your future self so don't worry you pulled through Queen! Forgive yourself, forgive those who attempt to dismantle you and allow the beauty that is life to re-enter the very part of you that will need to be resurrected.

Trust your worth because you are worthy. Never settle for anyone less than the King that will keep your crown atop your temple. You will have to wait for him but your wait will be worthwhile. Continue to dream that there will one day be a King that will find you, love you, adore you and make you his Queen. Believe, desire and expect *the one* that I can promise you God has especially created for you. Continue to watch love stories, read love stories and at times you may think that you will never find *that*. Keep being a Queen younger self because I pledge that true love does exist and not all of our opposites created are not bad. Remember that...

Take chances and be accepting. The world is full of opportunities that await you. It is so important for you to start young while you are an absorbing younger self. Be open to other ideas, cultures while staying true to who you are and where you come from. Never see color but look deeper into who a person is. Our color is simply given to us to make the world look more designed. Remember different doesn't make us better than another, it makes the world better because we are different. In a room full of the world, always expand your knowledge and never be afraid that you don't measure up. Remember every soul starts empty. Decide to fill your mind and body with everything you can feed on, that you can and will share with others. Never walk or run so fast ahead that you won't be able to reach back to help another walk and run with you. God's blessings for your life will never change how you're blessed. Giving what you have and know willingly blesses you more and unites us further.

Don't rush your growth. Take your age as it comes and embrace every single moment of just being young. Play outdoors, skip rocks in the water, get your brother in trouble, catch fireflies, make mud pies, sleep under the stars, tell scary stories at night, swing, get your knees scraped, ride bikes, sneak a piece of pie, talk about boys, have crushes, dance, swim in the lake, write in your diary, lay under trees, collect leaves, eat honeysuckles and crabapples, loose a tooth, have your first kiss, play dress up, get in a fight, build a playhouse, watch cartoons, drink Tang and just run arms wide open breathing fresh air for no reason at all. Live your pace. Know that these will actually be some of the best years of your life. You live once to be young and will die once when you are old.

Love and respect your parents. You will understand this more when you reach me. Listen to their guidance, their instructions and know that their words are from a place of nothing but genuine and true love. It will be hard sometimes to live with their decisions, the choices that they make for you but just trust your older self that it will all be valuable life lessons. I know you will muster up your mind to think that they just don't want you to grow up, that they don't want you to have any fun but reflect back to my words that they are this way because they want you *to live*. Thank them often, do your chores, be a good role model for your brother, give your best at everything and keep your room clean, well try to.

You are not alone. With God you are never alone. Always remember that, younger self. You will have one of many moments in your life when you will feel that it is you, that you are by yourself on this big planet. For each of those moments know He is with you to cover you. I am with you with loving arms around you. In those times, put on the Christopher Cross song *Sailing*, close your eyes, rest your feelings, take a deep breath and exhale. You have a whole family surrounding your existence that want you, younger self, to live.

I love you. I am so proud of who you have become, me. Never give up on what you know is yours. You were born for a purpose. Continue to strive for everything that God gave you the gift of. No matter how hard it may become, how many people may tell you to give up never ever stop believing in *who* you are. The universe needs you. When you get discouraged with thoughts that you can't make it, I want you to always remember one of your favorite things, a tree. It does not grow overnight, in a day but the growth of a tree is slow. It buries its roots deep and with water and sun it begins to grow. Soon, it will produce branches, then leaves and the deeper the roots are, the better the soil is, the more the tree will continue to grow. Be like a tree, younger self. Plant, root, grow, branch out and bloom! I'm waiting for you. The world is waiting for you.

Sheila Rena Bailey, better known as **Sheila B.**, is a Mother, Gege, published author, actress, filmmaker and director. Sheila is a survivor of sexual assault, domestic violence & cancer. Her passion is to empower with words, be a role model & educate Queens that they are crown worthy.

Chapter 2

In My Skin

Phalen D. Hendricks

I think it's about time that I finally told the truth. There's no easy way to really say such a thing, but it has to come out. The truth is that I used to hate being Black. I hated being in this skin every day, topped with my condition.

I hated everything about myself. I know that sounds pretty harsh, but it was a cold reality that I had to deal with. Even now I struggle at times with self-love, and it made me wonder if I was the only one who felt that way.

At times, I wondered if I was alone in my own loathing. However, as I grew up, I realized just how common a concept that it was, and to me, that's the problem. Why is it such a common concept for Black girls to hate their skin? Well, most girls like me, who grew up in the skin I did, more than likely have shared my experiences and know how it feels to be unequivocally Black and targeted for their blackness. That's what drove me to write this.

At 8 years-old, I came to the understanding that to a select few, black was an undesirable shade. Being a dark-skinned girl who was constantly criticized for her complexion begat a reality I was not mentally and emotionally prepared for. I was bullied by elementary school boys, probably with mothers and sisters with the same skin tone as mine. I was taught to hate my skin before I ever got the chance to experience it. I was already convinced, as a child, that I wasn't even enough for a Black man born from a similar mix. Imagine my confusion—how distraught and lost I became that I was being ridiculed for a skin tone that was also shared by a male counterpart.

One day in middle school, when I was simply minding my business and cracking jokes with friends, a boy in my class walked up to our table and randomly asked me: "Why are you so dark?" I didn't know how to respond. I was caught off guard. Was it not obvious why? Black mother, Black father. Black grandparents. It shocked and confused me that a male, equally as Black as I was, would ask me such a question. He compared me to charcoal and proceeded to laugh like the joke was funny—saying how I looked as if I was left out in the sun a little too long. Parts of me wish that I could exaggerate, but that day broke me a little more.

It hurt because I know that would never be a question he would have asked my two lighter-toned friends sitting beside me. He probably would have never thought of asking them that, but me? I was an easy target. I brushed it off in an attempt to ignore it, and went about the rest of my class with a smile, but that facade did not last for long. It took all that I had not to cry that day. My pride would not grant me the option to cry in front of him and give him the satisfaction to know that he hurt me that bad or that he affected my mentality in a way I never knew was imaginable. I tried to keep that same happy persona that I always branded, but even my friends could see that mask slowly cracking--revealing the little girl that had been tormented for six years for the very thing she despised. It made me feel even worse about myself and drove me even deeper into that depressive state I attempted to climb out of.

I never shook that feeling and those words have stuck with me ever since. There were days where I would search the internet for answers on how to lighten my skin, on how to appear like the "token Black girl" because apparently my skin and I didn't fit the bill. I searched and searched and the longer I searched, the more I lost myself, the more I despised and was revolted at the sight of my own flesh—to where I cursed my blood for making me "too dark". This was my reality, my life for 16 years. This is what it's like to be in my skin.

Knowing what I know now years later, I shouldn't have been surprised. The Black woman has been undervalued in all of America's very trying history. The most disrespected woman is the Black woman and even now such a statement rings true. How can it be that we, within our own communities, discriminate against our own? A group of women who have fought on the front lines and battled the enemy for their rights and their lives and STILL remain to be the target of hatred? The realization itself made me feel inadequate. I didn't feel pretty. I didn't feel loved. I didn't feel respected. Wanted. Valued. Appreciated. I felt nothing and that nothingness made me feel like I was nothing.

Even moving into high school, the only way I figured I would be noticed or even thought of was if I was lighter. I used to pray--foolishly--hoping that I could wake up in a different skin, so that I could stop feeling the way I did, so I could stop crying every night before school, so that I could live without the feeling of never feeling accepted. Don't be confused though, I never strived to be the center of attention; I just knew how it felt to be constantly overlooked as if I wasn't worth anything. I went through a quarter of my life hating the skin I was in because society taught me that I didn't fit into their fantasy. I quickly realized that young Black women like me were not a part of the party or meant to be celebrated. Hell, we couldn't even get in.

As Black women, we're forced to carry the burdens on our backs. Don't speak on it. Be silent. Speak too boldly and you're ghetto. Voice an opinion and you're bitter. Don't speak loud enough and you're weak. Say nothing and you're complicit.

Loud. Ghetto. Ratchet. Mean. Disrespectful. Angry. Bitter. Inconsiderate. Rude. Unattractive. I could think of more words that I've heard over the years if I wanted to. I could probably fill a dictionary with all the derogatory things that have been said about Black women. These are things that people use to define Black girls--dark skin girls like me. These are the words that some of the "men" we love so dearly, the men we fight for on a daily basis, use to describe us. That is the perception that they have of us and it's always the same. In the media, movies, and television shows, their views of Black women have never changed and those images have slowly crept into the cracks of our community at an alarming rate. It's an infestation that has taken the root of our people and molded it into something disgraceful.

Black girls have been placed at the end of the race before we even got to finish it in comparison to other races and skin tones. We've been made the butt of every joke to Black men who believe that even the most beautiful dark skin women are still inferior. It is a shame that we have to fight for recognition and value and a voice to speak our grievances to be accepted into the fold when in reality we shouldn't have to. There would be no fold without us. There would be nothing without the evolution of Black women and black ideals. The truth is the truth, there's no other way to say it that's digestible.

You may or may not be asking, "Well, how did you heal? How did you come to terms with your blackness?" If we're being honest, the past two years have been an enlightening experience for me. It has been a time of acceptance and pain, but also realization. Would I sound crazy to say that a movie of all things helped me love and appreciate my skin? It may not be a shock, but *Black Panther* made me love myself again. Seeing strong black women on the screen, standing beside equally strong men not as inferiors but as equals made me find value in myself. An all-Black cast, with Black producers, set designers, and writers. It allowed me to feel seen in a different light. It allowed me to come to terms with my blackness and celebrate myself for coming as far as I have. It let me have the moment to look back on my own family and the long line of strong Black women who helped raise me and forged the person that I am today. It helped me see that Black women are more than what we have always been made out to be. We are the creators and innovators, caretakers, and money makers we were made to be. And frankly, I don't need a man of any race or complexion to tell me that.

I used to hate being Black, but now I can't stand to think where I would be if I wasn't.

Phalen Denise Hendricks is an 18-year-old college student who was born and raised in Detroit, Michigan. In her youth, she moved to Atlanta with her elder sister and parents, where she grew a love for what she does now. She prided herself in her art as well as her writing, and became a semi-local figure on the popular publishing app known as 'Wattpad' when she was in middle school and has only perfected her craft after receiving her first 25,000 views on one of her oldest titles by the name of 'Unlove You'. She is a writer of many genres from Fantasy to Sci-Fi, Young Adult Fiction, Urban Fiction, and even Horror. The aspiring author taps into the deepest parts of her creative mind in an attempt to manufacture some of her own stories and develop a world that others can enjoy and get lost in as much as she does.

CHAPTER 3

The Evolution of "The Butterfly"

Necole F. Turner

There are a great many expectations placed on us. We are all things to all people and are often pulled into a hundred directions. We sometimes shoulder everyone's problems and serve as a sounding board to their ideas. Many times we are all things to the people in our lives. You are the confidante, the best friend, the therapist and companion. You are the strong one, so it seems, and the ever wise discerning spirit. But at what cost are we everything to everyone? The cost sometimes can be hefty. We are run down, worn down and broken down and out of options. Have you ever wondered how you functioned in the past with so many things on your to do list? I often wondered and thought that this type of time management was effective and limitless. Boy, was I wrong...so wrong.

I grew up in a household where children were seen and not heard. I didn't have an opinion and if I felt a certain way about any given thing, I learned to keep it to myself. I patterned my mood and behavior on how others felt. If someone was happy, I was happy. If someone was sad... you get the picture. I kept quiet in a corner holding my breath waiting on my father or my mother to walk in the door so I could adjust my mood accordingly. This carried over into my college days and even married life. I took on the persona of whomever was in my circle. I chose clothing, food and activities based on someone else's desires and wishes. Later, I would find this to be the unhealthiest thing that I could ever to do to myself.

I became an emotional eater to cope with the anxiety I felt. If I had a bad day, the first place I would run was Dairy Queen. Let me tell you that Peanut Butter Parfait and Blizzard was everything. When faced with the disappointments of life, I knew that I could turn to them and I would automatically feel better. They did not disappoint, talk back, give bad news or criticize. They were my friend. With the stresses of life pressing me, I ate to find comfort. Food became my coping mechanism. The problem was the very thing I thought was a friend quickly became my worst enemy. I eventually developed health issues, suffered from a self-conscious body image and anxiety. Yet I shared this with no one, I kept all this to myself.

Recognizing that I needed help, I started going to therapy. I found that I had to work on identifying and dealing with issues of failure and inadequacy. This helped me realize I didn't know who I was, why I was created or my reason for existing. Your reason for existing means something, it is your purpose. It is what you are meant to do each and every single day. Recently, I heard an interview with Matthew McConaughey and he shared that he didn't always know his purpose. He walked through life not having any direction. One day, he said that in a conversation with someone they recommended he write down all the things that he wanted to do in life. This stumped him, so he wrote down everything that he didn't want to do. This single exercise, he said, changed the trajectory of his life. Soon after, he got his first acting job. Therapy helped me realize that identifying your purpose is the key to feeling good about yourself. Feeling good about yourself can change how you see yourself, and how you see yourself can change your behavior. Fast forward 15 years and I have learned that my purpose is helping share the gift of knowledge with others on my growth journey.

Part of my continuing gift to myself is to meet with a group of individuals once a week in a Mastermind. It's a group where we get together in the COVID-19 environment via Zoom and share our accomplishments, challenges and opportunities. We chop it up in the virtual space and it can get down and real. We talk a lot about "mindfulness". This essentially focuses on being present in the moment and experiencing life based on your thoughts, ideas, perceptions and consciousness. The way we think and behave is dictated by three things: our environment; belief system; and any self-limited beliefs that we have about ourselves. For instance, if you want to start working out in the gym to be healthier, oftentimes we sabotage ourselves before we even get started. You look at your environment and see no one else in your family works out. Your belief system may force you to not take time for yourself because you need to help and serve others. Your self-limiting beliefs may tell you that you can't do certain exercises or you have too far to go.

The key to stopping this perception is retooling our minds. The conscious mind takes in a lot of information. What it doesn't use it dumps to the subconscious, the back of our mind. That subconscious mind will hold on to any information that it takes in because it can't recognize whether it is negative or positive. However, we tend to focus on the negative. Once a belief or idea has been accepted by the subconscious mind, it remains until it is replaced by another belief or idea. The longer a belief is held, the more it tends to become a fixed habit or thought pattern. This is how habits of action are formed, both good and bad. As a result, our mental habits become our physical behaviors. I learned this concept by studying the "24 Unconscious Rules of the Mind" and seeking an understanding of how to apply them in my life. It helped me tremendously in starting a new path in life because I learned how to stop repeating old patterns. You can't open a new door with old keys. We MUST break the habit of being ourselves and forge a new path.

Once you are on that new path, work to find your voice. Speak up. Know what you want out of life and go get it. Ask one more question, say that doesn't work for you and know what does. Set healthy boundaries and break circles where you don't see them practiced. We've spent enough time listening to other voices. Take this opportunity to hear your own. Our dreams are only manifested through how much we invest. Investing a small amount only gets a small return. That investment price initially may seem high but I can tell you the rate of return is immeasurable! Stop limiting your return and speak your DREAM! Make it known to others what you want to accomplish. I say this with a caveat attached. You won't be able to share your vision with everyone. Others won't be able to receive what you are telling them because it isn't their DREAM. It hasn't been spoken to them because it's not inside of them. Create the table and make your own rules.

Once I turned 40, I decided I wouldn't live by anyone else's standards. Trust me, this decision has been liberating, a cathartic moment that literally saved my life. I spent my 20's figuring out life and my 30's living someone else' life. I wanted to finally experience MY LIFE. So, I accepted the fact that I was going to make mistakes. Some of them were monumental but they were all my own. Now that I am approaching 50, I want to discover what else life has to show me. I am the co-orchestrator of my life. In order to be an offering to the world, we must become our own "I AM" and this comes from knowing our purpose. We spend our time trying to be the picture of perfection for others but we lose ourselves in the process. Accept that you aren't always going to get it right and be grateful for another opportunity to figure it out on your own terms. It will be an evolution of sorts, a project that will take a lifetime. The Book of Life speaks about "being perfected" until the day of completion. This is a continuous work that can't be rushed or circumvented. We have to go through this to become the greatest version of ourselves.

I say all that to say this… if I had known all that I know now, my journey would have been a little bit easier. I certainly would have made better decisions and been doing what I love a lot longer. I look back at the younger version of myself and write this:

"Dear Beautiful, you a revelation waiting to unleash your natural power that lies within you. You have been waiting to harvest what has been growing inside of you from the day you were born. It has always been there…trust it. Begin working now to expel those negative thoughts that fill your mind daily from the environment that surrounds you. That is not your home or your final destination. Those who cause you to doubt who you are and your purpose will fall away. They were not meant to take this journey with you. Remember, you are the true reflection of God's love design for your life…believe it. You are powerful beyond measure…harvest it. You are being perfected with every choice, every mistake and with every tear. Greater is coming…know it. Stop waiting for permission to be who you were born to be…embrace it. Everything you desire is waiting on the other side, just be willing to do the work to get there…SEE IT. The wind of change is behind you. Keep pushing and GO GET IT. I love you dearly, Necole. Be encouraged."

Sincerely,

The Butterfly.

Necole F. Turner is an Author and Podcaster. Her motto of "the best thing that we have to offer is the gift of knowledge to all we encounter" is something that applies in her everyday life. Her company "Innovative Butterfly" serves as a creative outlet for her writings and podcast, "The Beautiful Butterfly Project", which helps others develop strategies to empower themselves in life and in business. She has a Bachelor's Degree in Criminal Justice from Auburn University and a Juris Doctor from The Jones School of Law in Montgomery, AL. Affectionately known as "The Butterfly", Necole has been a keynote speaker, workshop facilitator and presents on topics such as women's empowerment, mindfulness and strategic goal setting. Her passion and heart's mission is to help educate entrepreneurs in business on the many aspects of protecting their work product and brand. Her passion and mission is also to help people know their purpose and its passionate pursuit as the host of "The Beautiful Butterfly Project" Podcast.

https://thebeautifulbutterflyproject.podbean.com/

I Thought You Should Know

Chapter 4

Ignorance, Friend or Foe

Beatrice M. Hunter

"Children should be seen and not heard."

I would like to think that the parents of my generation uttered these words out of concern for their children's innocence. Yet, I question the validity of the statement. My belief is our parents only wanted us to enjoy the benefits of childhood before coming face-to-face with the stark and harsh realities of our time. In the years to come, I would wrestle with the question of whether to include my children in the facts and decisions regarding survival and trials in our own lives. Could they understand? Finally, in their teens, I chose to be honest and arm them with the jagged sword of truth to hopefully assist them in the battles of their tomorrows.

As I look at my own life, I conclude that our parents had fostered a generation wherein ignorance was more of an unintended and oft unwelcome house guest, hardly ever a friend. We were instructed by our elders that "ignorance is bliss". Looking back, I do not recall a blissful interlude. My generation was taught not to ask questions, neither to listen to nor enter adult conversations. Some of us knew nothing and thought that was the way it was supposed to be. I had some "real" growing up to do, and the time came faster than I expected.

Let me tell you about my childhood. My adolescent to teen world consisted of a five by five box of city blocks, a village like community called Tinbridge Hill. For as long as I can remember, this was as far as I could venture alone in my hometown of Lynchburg, Virginia. (I will venture to answer that question that just popped into your mind about the name of my town later). I must confess that there were times when the urge to know more caught me, and I would practically tiptoe out of my mandated secure community, even then feeling vulnerable any place else other than Tinbridge Hill. Everyone in that box knew and protected me, even from myself. Through my shielded ignorance, I had no idea that the entire world did not look at me the same as everyone else. I did not know that in many places outside the box, severe harm could befall me simply because I was a Black child, a descendant of slaves, turned maids and always servants. It was truly the start of my education when I left Virginia in the early 70s and moved to New York.

The 70s in New York was a tumultuous period of rioting, picketing, and protesting for civil rights. I had not heard anything about this in Lynchburg, and upon witnessing it, all I could feel was pity for those "colored" folks up there. These northerners were rebelling because they seemed to want white people to accept them. I somehow managed to avert their attention once they learned where I came from. "You come from Lynchburg?" they exclaimed, as if I could not have been from a worse place. "Is that where they hang niggahs at?" They burst into laughter. I became defensive at that point. "No, they don't do that anymore," I retorted, not realizing until much later how utterly ignorant I had sounded. I had heard about how some college kids had refused to leave a drug store on our Main Street. Evidently, the owner refused to serve them, but white people were in the group so they must have done something wrong, hadn't they? After all, they had gotten arrested. It was just that in Lynchburg, we (Blacks) could always go to the restaurants and stores we wanted to. True, we had to stand at the counters and order our food to go or stand outside at a window at curb service. One such place we called Tip Tops. I recall that whether it was an adult or one of us children, we had to stand at the window and wait our turn. I remember peering thru the hazy and dirty window at the white patrons inside, sitting at the counter, eating, or drinking, laughing, and having fun. After a while when we had failed to get the waitress' attention, one of the patrons eventually pointed in our direction at the window. She must have known we were standing there; she had motioned for us to go around the side when we forgot and came to the door. On other days when we got there and she was busy, she yelled out, "Window closed!" If a parent was with us, she explained to our parents that even though the window was open, it was only open for ventilation and not for service. And to me, that was fine. In fact, I was a bit embarrassed that we had disturbed her while she was so busy. These New York people must have it so much harder.

For my first couple of years in New York, I found myself defending the practices of a Jim Crow system to my northern cousins. Of course, I didn't know it then that I ardently defended segregation, bigotry and inequality. It was just the way things were down in the south. Yes, I gave my newly found friends a chuckle or two as I bragged about how in the south, we all got along, how they ought to be ashamed mocking the name of the man that had founded our town, Mr. John Lynch. I remember someone asking me, "Why do you think they call the town Lynchburg? It's because they did lynch niggas there Bea!" How utterly foolish I felt since these encounters. My naiveté and ignorance spoke much too loudly. Unknowingly, I had defended the Lynch Movement. Lynchburg had been named after John Lynch, the brother of the man who had devised a way to permanently punish his enemies during the Revolutionary war by hanging them... Charles Lynch, John's brother. And yes, Blacks had been lynched in our town. In fact, the first electric chair of Virginia had been tested in Lynchburg. I shudder to think today, how many Black bodies had swung from those old Oak trees I climbed during my childhood or sat beneath. How many white families had held a picnic while viewing the hanging of a Black man or woman, maybe even a child? Picnics were synonymous with "pick - a – nigga". That is where the word had originated. Had ignorance been this child's friend or foe? For me, childhood had been a blank slate for the education the world would surely supply, and it filled so quickly. I asked myself many times, would I have been better armed for today had I known, or would I have self-destructed? Did I self-destruct? I wonder...

Beatrice M. Hunter is a mother of an African American King, and Queen, a grandmother of noble nine, and great grandmother of five royals. Her family's nobility was not granted by man, but by being born African American and the higher power of us all. Her desire is to leave a legacy for her offspring and those to come through genealogical research. Beatrice's passion is researching local history and imparting whatever lessons she has learned to the youth of today. She has been blessed to have various articles published in local venues, give talking sessions to college students, and is currently writing two book.

I Thought You Should Know

Chapter 5

The Ugly Cries

Nicho Charisse

This letter is for the future daughters, sisters, mothers, grandmothers, and female leaders. Before I dive into these words, let me start with first letting you know that you are beautiful, gorgeous, pretty, phenomenal, smart, needed, wanted and enough.

As you grow into womanhood, you are going to encounter many things. Your first heartbreak, the birth of a child, the loss of a loved one, or an award that you have worked extremely hard for. Tears are a way that we communicate and show our emotions. Just like with a picture, they tell many stories and talk a thousand words.

However, society has considered crying a sign of weakness and vanity is strength. You may be told to never let them see you cry or not to cry because you will mess up your makeup. You need to always look your best. You are to get over it and get over yourself. Well, this letter is to let you know that you can cry ugly. You can show your emotions. You can let the world know that you are angry, happy, or hurting. Women are very emotional beings. There is nothing that we can do about it. That is how we were created. Do not give your emotions rules. How your tears fall is how they fall.

No matter the era, women wear many hats. We are the nurturers. We are not just mothers to the children we bear but also the neighbors' children, the kids in schools, or a child we may see in passing that just needs guidance. We are the spouse that makes sure our better half is ok even when we are not. We are the first one to wake up in the morning and the last one to go to sleep at night. We are the boss, the leader or CEO and still handle home. We try to take burdens off everyone else though we may already be stressed. We say, "Yes" when we should be saying "No". It can be overwhelming. People forget you have a life, a heart and you are tired. Do not stop those tears from falling. Stop looking in the mirror and scolding yourself because your foundation is streaked. Do not feel guilty about needing a break and releasing everything that is on your heart and quieting your spirit. Go ahead and be ugly. It is ok.

I understand that there are going to be those who will tell you what I am communicating is wrong. This may come from your acquaintances (your real friends will not tell you that), your mom, your boss, and men. That may be how they were raised. They are already conditioned to have what is called a tough skin. The more you hold in what is tugging at your heart the harder it is to heal. The more you listen to everyone and not your own heart the more you will lose yourself.

You are not the only one who will be wrestling with this. Watch and observe your sisters in your path. It may be a stranger, but she is still your sister (in Christ, in spirit, etc.). While you are looking at her beautiful outfit, high heels, and the walk of authority, make sure you watch her smile and look in her eyes. Compliment her but also let her know that you are her sister, and you are there for her. Let her know that she is beautiful and it is ok to cry. Never judge your sisters with no makeup or makeup smeared, wig crooked, barefoot, heels broken, shoe strap broken button lost, zipper broke, bonnet or scarf leaning to the side with strands of her hair sticking out. Do not assume she is looking rough on purpose. Do not look at her with disgust or with a twisted mouth of judgement. The first thing that comes to your mind should not be, "She has no friends", or "Who let her out of the house?" That could be you. It probably has been you. Instead, walk over to her, have a seat, reach into your purse, and pull out a handkerchief. If you do not have one, consider purchasing some. Conversations do not always have to start with "Hello" and you do not have to tell her your name. Just pass her the handkerchief. This could go a few ways. She may thank you. She may begin to wipe her tears. She may talk to you. Ignore how she looks (unless she may need some type of coverings) and worry about her heart. As you talk, you may find out that you need her as much as she needs you. Do not give her a mirror. Wipe her tears and fix her mascara while you are talking. The handkerchief is for her to keep so that she may wash it and treasure it to remember the sister that got her through a bad day or to pass it to the next woman to wipe her tears. If you are a man reading this letter by chance, keep a handkerchief in your pocket to wipe a daughter's tears, a mother's cries and to wipe away a woman's grief. Your sister does not have to be someone you know. This is one of the ways we build women up and not tear them down. We open our hearts to one another other, let them cry and check on them later.

Please, do not get me wrong, I know there may be times that you will not always be able to show those tears at certain occasions, but do not just do it. Do not hold it in. Do not ignore what you may be going through. Create yourself a prayer room, find a storage closet, lock the bathroom door, and decompress. If you need to reach out and receive help, do that. There is nothing wrong with talking to a therapist or seeking spiritual guidance. Call someone you trust who will be an ear and wipe your tears. Do not ever be ashamed of needing help. We all need it sometimes. Pull off those lashes, hang that wig on the rack, kick off those shoes, turn on the gospel/R&B/(t)rap/jazz or whatever you are feeling at that time and let it flow. If you are like me and cannot carry a tune with a shopping cart, so what, sing anyway. Sing, scream and yell your heart out if it helps you. Do not worry about what you look like. Who is going to check you? If someone has something to say, they can leave.

Have an Ugly Girls Night. The only rule is to only invite those you trust, ladies who are willing to listen, ladies whom you consider your sister friend and understand that what is discussed and the emotions that may follow must stay within those walls. Do not make it all about tears. Have games, drinks, and food. Everyone wears fun pajamas, and make sure you have handkerchiefs on hand.

I hope this letter will help you on your journey in life. If you find this helpful to you, pass it to the next woman... along with a handkerchief, or save it for the next generation. Now, go have a good ugly cry.

Love always,

Nicho Charisse

Nicho Charisse is a resident of Pittsburgh, Pennsylvania. This is her fourth collaboration book. Her writings have also appeared in *Reflections on Purpose*; *Dear Depression*; and *In the Morning*. Nicho enjoys creating worlds through her writing and helping people escape their realities.

I Thought You Should Know

Chapter 6

Dear Young Single Black Mother

nA' Stubbs

Dear Young, Single, Black Mother,

Wow! What a ride, huh? Sitting in the backseat of the lives of the adults who have taken on the task of rearing you, taking in more than what a little girl with an underdeveloped level of understanding probably should. As you look out of the "backseat" windows…of your soul… watching THIS one and THAT one and that OTHER one pass by, you unintentionally take note. But only the "future" knows what you will do with all the notes that you have taken. Given the cards you have been dealt, I'm confident you will do what needs to be done with them.

Once upon a time, you thought life was as normal as normal could get. Once upon a time, all you wanted to be was a "regular" kid with a "regular" life, filled with cartoons, play dates, bedtime stories, and summer vacations…hide and seek, happy meals, monkey bars, fun dip, and mud pies (not at the same time of course, LOL)…baby dolls, hand games, roller skates, hopscotch, the ice cream man and double-dutch with barrettes and ballies…that speak the language of a little black girl in the pure essence of her fun. CLACK! CLACK! CLICKETY CLICKETY! CLACK! CLACK!

Not until you were older did you hardly even recognize, let alone feel, the absence of your father, the man who helped to create you, and could have contributed so greatly in the security of your being, but consciously chose not to. "Doesn't everyone live with their mother… and ONLY their mother?" was the unasked question that shaped your view of the world, the neighborhood, the community that you were developed in. By age 10, you hardly ever saw YOUR mother, due to her two and a half jobs that she worked to provide sustenance for you and your four younger siblings. In her defense, I must say, she only did what she knew to do. She only "knew to do" from what she watched her OWN mother do to raise her and HER siblings. I know, at times you felt like you WERE her, as you rose daily at 5 a.m. to take care of business, a business that was not necessarily yours to take care of. Tending to your siblings... you woke them up, dressed them, fed them, washed and combed their hair, wiped their noses (and sometimes little butts), delivered them TO and retrieved them FROM school, defended and protected them... as often as necessary, helped with homework, put them to bed, and all within only a 24-hour period. This, not leaving many hours for yourself. This, forming the habit of an all-day yawn. Parentification! Yep it is a real word, and you, My Sweet, were the epitome of it. While it was not by choice... YOUR choice that is...you would have it no other way when it came to looking out for your siblings. But who was looking out for you? Who woke YOU up, dressed YOU, fed YOU, washed and combed YOUR hair, wiped YOUR nose, delivered YOU TO and retrieved YOU FROM school, defended and protected YOU, helped YOU with YOUR homework, put YOU to bed? YOU... that's who.

When it came to looking out for yourself, sometimes you just wished you did not have to learn so much on your own. Sometimes, you just wished that you had visits from others of your own age who could remind you of just how old you WERE NOT. Sometimes, you just wished that someone would have asked if YOU needed or wanted anything, which would denote that YOU TOO were being "taken care of". Sometimes, you just...

Yeah, sometimes.

But through it all, you never complained. I wish someone would have told you that through it all, your character was being built. I wish someone would have told you that through it all, your knowledge of self and others was being formed. I wish someone would have told you that through it all, you were being introduced to your sense of survival. I wish someone would have told you that through it all, the very elements of everyday life were preparing you for your own life that was to come. But who knew? Who knew that your mother would become a grandmother in her early thirties? Who knew that your young siblings would become young aunties and young uncles? Who knew that in the years where you should be planning for your eighth grade promotion that you would be planning a baby shower instead? But even in all that was unknown, I just wish someone would have told you that through it all, they were proud of you.

At age 12, I asked you, "What do you want to be when you grow up?"

Unsurprisingly, young, single, black mother never made the list

Especially since you were always one who communicated with boys with your fists

In fact, your fist spoke so loudly, I thought you would never even be kissed

Haha!

Let alone...

At 15, YOU told me...

"I swear it feels like young and single mother hood snuck up on me."

You said...

"It is as if one day I was living my OWN life and the next I was living as someone ELSE in a movie."

I watched you go from book bags, pencils, notebooks, homework…

Spelling bees, S.A.T.'s and algebra

To diapers, strollers, cribs, pacifiers…

Car seats, bottles, and baby formula

From school dances, field trips, cutting class, and detention

To 3 month checkups, 29 hour days, inexplicable emotions

And not to mention…

…looking ahead to at least 18 more years of the unknown

You expressed, "I couldn't even plan a successful future of MY OWN."

"So how? Why? Have I been entrusted with another life…

Technically I'm "chronologically challenged" and this just does not seem right

I am so proud of you for taking responsibility

Proud of you recognizing that in your own choosing of the color, material

And size of YOUR comforter and sheets

You are willing to lay in the bed that YOU have made

No matter how comfortable or UN-comfortable it may be

In a world, a society that does not respect a single black young mother's voice

One that has spoken FOR you since the introduction of your existence

I hear your strength in all that you DON'T say

And your daily press to get this thing as "right" as you can is a far greater evidence

With certainty I encourage you that this is not the end of the world

As you are surrounded by women who have survived the jungles of single motherhood

Women who have survived the struggle and sacrifices of their own lives

To ensure that they've done everything that they could...

To raise children who value the early years of education

To aid them in one day being a prominent figure

Helping to shape the better parts of this nation

To encourage their children to be secure in their independence

To seek a foundation and a significance in what is relevant

To hold a pride in what they deem is their faith

To cherish the richness and strength of their phenomenal race

To believe in themselves so deeply that they can never be denied

To instill in them that they can accomplish any goal to which their true efforts are applied

There are oh so many things that you have to look forward to teaching your seed

Even though most of it you will probably be learning together

At your age, you are still very much an impressionable student yourself

Putting it frankly my dear, the space behind your ears "can't get no wetter"

HaHa!

But seriously…

Once you are able to get over the guilt and fear of your predicament

Once you are able to take a step back and look

It is my hopes that you will be able to clearly see

That there are all types of people surrounding you on this path that you took

YES

Some will be there to condemn, stereotype, and log you as a statistic

Those you must quickly resolve

That in YOUR life, THEIR say does not fit

I would like to direct your attention to those around you

With knowledge AND wisdom to teach you a few thousand things or two

About life and doing what SHOULD be done

As opposed to you just settling for "doin' wat chu GOTTA do"

No time to sit, do nothing, and focus on

What it is that you feel you've done so wrong

Use the "weight" that's been added to your life

As a tool to continue to make you strong

I am looking forward to watching the journey of how you will mature

And not just settle for getting older

How you will far surpass expectations and thoughts
Of you being just another
Young, Black, Single mother
I am… WE are… rooting for you, baby!
Love,
Mothers Who "SEE" You and Are Encouraged By You

nA' Stubbs is the Founder/Artistic Director of uNiqu' Performing Arts & The No More! Project. Over her 17 years of artistic delivery through uNiqu' she has penned numerous stage plays, songs, spoken word pieces, and a myriad of other written works, lying in wait for life to be "breathed" into them.

Chapter 7

Pearls of Life

Lynn Renee Means

WISDOM OF OUR ELDERS...LEARN TO LISTEN
I found there to be a wealth of wisdom and knowledge when we spend time with our elders. They have learned patience and have the time to nurture us... if we allow them to. In addition, we bless them with our presence and care. The wisdom our elders bring to the table can be of great comfort to our lives. My grandmother gave me the intimacy I needed as a kid although at the time I did not recognize it. She taught me to knit and crochet. I learned to sit and talk with her. She was always teaching me something. Be patient with our elders they have much to share.

Listening can be difficult at times while moving through the journey of life because things can move quickly and appear that we only have time to focus on what we are going through. This can cause us to miss out on appreciating the good things in our lives. We often end up giving too much of our thought life over to our problems. I had very few people in my life when I was young who encouraged me or was able to help me see myself in a positive light. I wanted to grow and would listen to my elders and others who I thought were moving in a positive direction. Learning to listen can save us a lot of wrong turns and heartaches.

I visited my grandmother during the summers in the south (hot south), running and playing, going from one friend's house to another. Sometimes my grandmother wouldn't let me go anywhere. She'd say, "You stay home today and be still." This was difficult for me to understand. I could go no further than the front porch and have no company. I was so busy being mad because all I did was look out the window most of the time. But I remember that it gave me time to think and take things in more. I paid more attention to nature and the lightning bugs at night. I am not saying you need to go as far as my grandmother did, but make quiet time a part of your life. It is an important part of the listening process.

As an adult, I am grateful for having that experience of being still. I now love quiet time. When I would talk to others about quiet time, they would say, "I don't like the quiet or being still. I need to have something going on around me, music, tv, social media or just being on the go." If you are the type of person who struggles with the quiet, it would help you to practice sitting quietly until you become comfortable with it. It will change your life. It is important to hear from the voice within you. I believe that space is where God speaks to us.

Our elders are the strength and the fiber that hold our families together and should be held in high esteem.

When I think of what I thought I knew, I did not know much at all. But I was committed to learning. I remember my mother telling me how things were, and I thought that was in her day, not my generation. That old time stuff does not apply, I thought. I was wrong. Regardless of what changes are made in relationship to time, like clothes, hair, activities, etc., some things stay the same. The wrong mindset will lead to wrong decisions.

No one knows everything, but the truth will bear witness with your soul. Do not go against it just because it does not fit in with what you want.

OPPORTUNITES ARE NOT ALWAYS EVIDENT... TAKE A CLOSER LOOK

Look for the opportunities around us. We must recognize them and reach out and take advantage of them. Even in our youth, opportunities are all around us. Sometimes the noise around us will cause us to miss them.

When I was around 10 years old, I lived in a rough neighborhood with a lot of fights and unhappy people. I did not realize it then, but it was a result of people not loving themselves. To love yourself is to love your neighbors.

I had a neighbor (my friend) whose mother was strict, so I thought. Her kids were not allowed to come outside and play with the other neighborhood kids. But she allowed me to come to their home to visit them. They knew how to play the piano and were teaching me to play. I really started to get the hang of it but lost interest because I did not like the discipline and wanted to be outside with the other kids. This was a missed opportunity for me, especially having no other outlets except to hang out with the neighborhood kids like me who also had no real guidance in their lives to truly uplift them. It is ironic. I love music and I had a few opportunities in my life to have free lessons from some incredibly talented people. I could have learned to play drums and piano. The noise in our daily lives can speak louder than the opportunities around us.

Focus is key. Teach your children at a young age how to focus. This can be done, I believe, through intimate conversations and teaching them discipline and about quiet time. Reading is important also. It can show and tell them more than they will learn in their current situation and give them a mindset to dream and hope.

CHALLENGE YOUR INSECURITES

Your greatness can overcome your insecurities if you can connect with your authentic self. The earlier you can find out who you are, the earlier you can begin to grow and balance your life. The longer you live without exploring who you are, the longer you will feel like an impostor at most things that you do. I tried to tell myself that just because I said I was not insecure and I was confident that speaking these things would mean I was ok. But the things I said really did not change my insecurities or my lack of confidence. What changed it all for me was to find my truth, to admit that I was insecure and lacked confidence, and to deal with why I felt that way. No one is perfect and pretending that you are will only make it more difficult to deal with the fact that you are not. Look at it this way, we all have challenges and need to bring about change in our lives to do better. Doing better will get us closer to the greatness that we are.

There can be sadness in life but there is much happiness too. I could not see how my insecurities caused me not to see the better side of me. My direction in life would have been different with the proper influence and a healthy image of myself. In the 1950s and the 1960s it was tough for me being of dark skin and female. Kids, of course, can be cruel and were relentless at teasing me. Adults as well. Some of the things said would hurt me to my soul.

I remember when a song came out by the Godfather of Soul James Brown called "Say it Loud, I'm Black and I'm Proud", something snapped in me. It was the first time I had something to say back to those who teased me. I would wail that line "I am black, and I am proud!" What a difference a song can make. It is a testament to how much influence positive words can have whether they are spoken or sang in a song. If you did not have what you needed to grow in a balance and healthy way, forgive yourself for mistakes you made because of some of your decisions. You do not know what you do not know. Now, when you know better, you must do better. Your destiny depends on it.

"To know what I know now..." How many times have you heard the statement? I have heard it many times in my life but only after living for many years did I really understand what that statement really meant. Hindsight really is 20/20.

ALLOW LOVE TO BE YOUR GUIDE

I thought I knew what love was about. I thought love was a euphoric feeling, like butterflies in my stomach, however, I noticed I did not feel this way all the time, which made me wonder more about love and what it really was. If love is simply about feelings, we would be all over the place.

To love is to do what's right by others and yourself, love also has pure motives. There are many things you will want to do in life. Let love be the center and you will be less stressed and less anxious. Love will bring balance to your life. You will hear some people say some people are un-loveable. When you understand love is not about feeling only, you can love them. Love is strong not weak. Love will build your character and overcome the things in your life that try and hold you hostage to your ego. Make love your foundation.

Give people the space to grow and find themselves. So often when people do not think the same things we think, believe what we believe, behave the way we think they should, we cast them away. Later, when we evolve, we find that our judgment of them was unfounded and that their thought had merit. It can be hard sometimes not to judge others, but we must work on that flaw. It is flawed because you cannot really know what is in someone's heart, that space is reserved for God to judge. We are not capable of judging someone's heart regardless of how great we think we are.

After all the things I suffered, I came to the realization just how precious life is. Even during challenging times, you can still feel the intrinsic beauty of the quality of life. Long suffering can seem unfair. Learn the fruit of love, it can make the struggles in your life easier to handle. Patience must be worked in our lives. If we can learn and apply patience, we can control how hard hit we will be by the circumstances we might find ourselves in life.

To those who are trying to figure out life's journey, go in peace. Life is too short to not take time to process and find ways to enjoy it. Find love in your heart and pay it forward, this will make the world a better place.

JUST MY THOUGHTS

Time in the rearview mirror becomes a memory. A memory is past tense. When time has been unkind to you, know that NOW is always the opportunity to create new memories. Keep the positive memories before you. We are blessed to have the power to recall memories that can help to inspire and uplift us when we need it. You have the power within yourself to chart your own path. Memories are one of the superpowers that can help you.

Lynn Renee Means is an author, speaker and coach. She is a woman of compassion, vision and purpose, shining a light on self-empowerment and healing. A mother, wife, daughter and friend, Lynn has more than 20 years of experience as a mentor, empowerment coach and pastor. She produced and hosted the radio talk show, The Soul Speaks, and co-founded and pastored Higher Ground World Outreach Ministries. Her hobbies include interior design, videography, reading and, gardening. She and her husband reside in Atlanta.

I Thought You Should Know

Chapter 8

Hidden Truth

Heaven Hightower

My name is Heaven Hightower. I am a black 15-year-old girl and I am a public figure in Atlanta, Georgia. I haven't experienced any racial encounters in life yet, but what the news and social media has shown me differs. Every day on the news I hear another black life lost, from murder, police brutality, gun violence, and more. I see riots on social media platforms around the world and protests about police brutality and how the criminal justice system is corrupted.

Remember the pledge of allegiance? "…and justice for all"? I recited it from kindergarten through 5th grade and then stopped. I've wondered why, but nowadays the answer is in the world. When I hear the word, "Black", I hear so many things…Power, Skin Color, Injustice… They range from good and bad. I went to meet ups about Black Live Matter causes. I've even had the chance to speak to a crowd of people my age and older about the younger point of view, how we learn and how things affect us. I have also starred in the movie, *The Hate U Give*, based on a fictional book by Angie Thomas. The movie was a bout a girl named Starr and the current state of police and the Black community relations. My character, Natasha, appears in a flashback scene. THUG LIFE = The Hate U Give Little Infants Effs Everybody. Tupac

What you put out in the world, infants will remember that and copy the older person who is the one the younger people look up to. Knowing your rights is importance in life. I come from a family of hard work and success. I come from a household filled with sweat and humbleness. My mother inspires and motivates me. She tells me to never give up. I am a Black girl in a world of gun violence and lost lives, but also of bringing about justice from the injustice. Black people are considered a threat to the justice system, and are considered weak-minded. But as the youth and as a Black girl in America, I am here to change that and show that I can and we can do and be anything we desire. Everything I do, from school, modeling, acting, and other things, is to prove the system wrong. I also try to show my mom and family that I can be successful and they support me and help me strive for greatness.

I am multi-talented, but I am also human. I like Tik Tok, singing, and dancing. Although I am serious about my work, behind the scenes I am as silly as Eddie Murphy. I am striving to major in art/design in my future college, Savannah College of Art and Design (SCAD). I want to be a fashion designer and continue to model, act, and more. I help my community with my foundation, Heaven Help One, Help All Foundation Inc. I help families in need of food, clothes, and other necessities. I love to travel. I love to learn. My two favorite subjects are English language arts and biology. My weakness is the tests. Even when I do well on the quizzes, I still struggle on the tests. But I'm working to improve that. My strength is talking, working hard, and showing dignity in my work. I used to hate talking to my teachers. My mother would do that for me. But I am at the age and grade where I am becoming a mature young lady. I was also an extremely independent scholar. I wouldn't ask for help on anything. But now, if I have a question, I ask and my teachers help me resolve my problems.

My goal is to continue to grow as a student. I desire to be a STAR (Safe. Thoughtful. And Respectful), salutatorian, or valedictorian.

My mom has two kids, my big brother and me. My brother graduated from high school and went to college, and I want to do the same. I am a scholar eager to learn, and to succeed. I love my dad as well. He is very intelligent and an artist. He likes to teach me from home more in depth of things and he pushes me to be great just like my mother. I love my family, friends, teachers, and other people I've come across along my journey.

God is the biggest reason I stay grounded. No one's perfect and I loved every time I failed because I learned and did better. Overcoming obstacles and learning from my mistakes will help me succeed in high school and beyond.

I am Black and I am proud. I love my skin color and who I am. I love my culture, history, and background. I represent the kids in the movement. During this Coronavirus pandemic, we talk about civil rights, when it seems like we don't even have human rights as Black people. We are still considered 3/5th human... since the clause was put in the United States Constitution in 1787! But I didn't learn that in school. I didn't learn real Black history. Yeah, his-story, like Columbus discovered America when Native Americans were already here. My family has fought and died in every war for America, but still a lot of us are treated less than human. It makes me feel neutral because yes, we are fighting for our people and rights and at the same time they sometimes get out of control and cause commotion that leads to shooting. For example, here in Atlanta, 8-year-old Secoriea Turner was shot July 4 near the Wendy's where a police officer killed Rayshard Brooks. We got work to do... all of us!

Heaven Hightower is a young influencer in Atlanta and around the world via social media. At 15, she is already an accomplished actor, model, author, and philanthropist. She has appeared in such productions as *The Hate U Give*, *The Darkest Minds*, and *Daytime Divas,* and is author of Heaven's Life on the Runway, a coloring, activity and motivational book. Heaven is also founder of Heaven Help One, Help All Foundation Inc., an organization that serves the less fortunate. In her spare time, she enjoys singing, dancing and spending time with family and friends.

I Thought You Should Know

Chapter 9

Life Through My Eyes

Kamryn Denise Johnson

Today is what seems like my hundredth attempt at trying to write this. Trying to figure out what I want to write, how I want to write. But then, as I was thinking about it, a new question came to me. *Why* am I writing this? It's pretty sad, don't you think? I'm here, writing a story about my life as a Black American, the struggles I've gone through, the racism I had to experience as a child, as a teen or even now as a young adult. I shouldn't have to. No one should have to, but here we are. Me... writing about it and you reading it. Seems like nothing has changed, huh?

Growing up, I could say the cliché 'I didn't see color' because, well I didn't. I didn't pay attention to the color of someone else's skin. Whether they were lighter than me or darker than me, all I cared about was making friends. Frankly, if I'm being truthful, I didn't even understand the concept of race, ethnicity, nationality or any of it. But what I failed to realize was that others did. I had my first racial experience somewhere around fifth grade, maybe age 10 or 11. There were only three other Black kids in my class and I didn't realize at the time but, our teacher had always chosen us to pick on. We were always getting in trouble for things we hadn't even done. We got odd looks and stares. I never stressed, though, never wondered why, never asked why. To me, it was what it was.

It wasn't until I hit middle school that I start learning to see the world in a different light. I wasn't protected by the innocent child mind anymore. I started seeing kids my color, got a cell phone, learned about the world of the internet, learned about my skin and my history. But also, I learned that the boys of my race, didn't like the girls of our race. I watched as my crushes only picked the girls that were blonde or brunette with the glowing blue eyes or the light brown ones, yet they downplayed the girls who had the same darkened complexion as them. They constantly made fun of the beautiful dark skin girls regardless of their beauty because they weren't made of the same pale complexion as the other girls they had passed around among their friends. It was sick, it was sad. Thinking about how that became the new normal to their girls, when they deserved nothing but the same compliments that the other girls were getting.

As I entered high school, racism and colorism became very prominent in my eyes. I started to see it everywhere I went, heard it, read about it. I saw just how disgusting people were in this world. Whether I was getting odd and disgusted looks from older white people, or if I heard our own Black men tell our Black women that she's 'too dark' for him or that she's 'pretty for a dark skin girl'. But learning this also made me learn that I had something called 'light-skin privilege', meaning I wasn't 'too dark' to grab the attention of a guy, or I wasn't being completely disrespected, but still wasn't pale enough to keep the attention or to not be called 'ghetto' for just being who I was.

The colorism that dark skin women face from people of all races and genders is absolutely sickening. I always ask myself, why does it bother people so much? They would hate it if someone talked that way about their mom, daughter, sister, auntie, grandmother, etc. So why would they be putting this hurt onto someone else. Is it self-inflicted? Is it a hate thing within themselves? What prompted them to act this way? They would probably say, 'it's my preference' as if their preference validated them tearing down someone's confidence, make them hate themselves and want their complexion be lighter. Each and every girl should know she is beautiful, regardless if she is light or dark. It does not matter and no one has the right to tell them anything different. They love the white girls for acting as if they were us, but hated the skin color that comes with us.

Does that make sense to you? Black women get frowns for box braids, saying they're unprofessional, but when white women do it, it's now 'cute'. Why is it that we have to submit to the white ways of society? Straighten our hair because that's what they see as 'professional'. This way of thinking has broken down the confidence of many young Black girls we know today where they've had to shield or hate their blackness because of how this country was founded. For years, I've worn my hair straight and because of that, I truly don't even know how to properly style my natural hair, which has been damaged by the nine years of heat damage. There are little Black girls in the world who hate their hair because it may be 'too curly' or 'too kinky'. I remember once telling my mom that, 'I wish I had white people's hair because it's easier'. I hated the long process that took up the weekend. But soon enough, I learned that I did not want white people hair, whether my hair was straightened or not. I taught myself to love my hair no matter what. These young girls need to be taught to love themselves, their hair, their skin color, their heritage, their everything.

The disrespect of being a woman added on with the disrespect of being Black, makes us the most hated species on this here earth. Even with some support, the disrespect will always hurt. It will always break someone down. It will always harm someone's confidence. It will always have a permanent hold on somebody's life. I am inspired by the Black women in this world because it's not easy to be us. I would dare anyone of the opposite races and gender to walk in the shoes of a Black woman for just a day. Someone out there probably is saying, 'easy enough' and wouldn't make it an hour. Honestly, no male of any race would survive being a woman, period. For example, the catcalling and constantly getting downplayed for things that are for men. Who are they to tell us that? To tell anyone that?

Truthfully, I haven't had much experience with either racism or colorism. I have been very fortunate to not have experienced it as much as other Black men and women have. I truly believe that this world needs a major change. It's 2021, let's show love and not hatred. Black people are not the enemy. Black women are not your enemy. If anything, we would be your most supportive allies if allowed. Stop the disrespect to the women who birthed you, who raised you, who has shown an unlimited amount of support, who will stand by you. Don't feel threatened because we speak our minds and don't let anyone just run over us. Respect us because we do it. Respect us because we respect you. Racism may always be a factor, but the colorism in our own community needs to stop. Love one another. Support one another because at the end of the day, nobody is gonna understand our struggle like we do. We are all we have. This world is divided enough as it is. Don't give it another reason to be divided even more. I love us. Black Lives Matter.

Kamryn D. Johnson was born and raised in the California Bay Area, where she spent most of her life bouncing around to different cities with her family, even still at the young age of 19. As a lover of fiction and the supernatural, Kamryn took a liking to many of America's most popular teenage shows that influenced her and her love for literature. Developing writing as her hobby, the young author used writing as an escape from her life because of her feeling as if she never had a secure home to be in. Finding solace in the relationship, she created between her characters that she both read and wrote about, giving her a true feeling of home. She used her talent for storytelling by turning her feelings into short stories for others to read and indulge in.

Chapter 10

A Letter from One Black Queen to Another

Dezire Moore

Hello Black Queen!

How are you doing? Never mind your response because I already know all too well your answer... "I'm ok." Yeah, I already knew because it sounds all too familiar. If you think that's something, check these out: "Yes, I'm sure. I'm ok. I'm fine. No I got it. I don't need any help. I'm fine. There's nothing wrong with me. No, I'm not crying. It's just my allergies acting up." Sounds familiar? Yes, I know, you too? Always be strong no matter what, repeated lies from a strong Black woman.

I'm writing this letter because I thought you should know it's ok to turn in your cape and say I'm not a superhero. It's ok to say no. It's ok to say I need help. It's ok to say no, I'm not ok. Through the decades Black women have been portrayed to always be strong and to never be bothered. We were portrayed as to not have any type of emotion, "just suck it up, you'll be alright." We were taught to stand on our own two feet. "You don't need any help; that makes you seem weak." These were the things taught to me growing up, passed down from generation to generation as a blessing or a curse. No, I just can't take on this type of strength anymore. I'm tired and it's time for me to be honest with myself and to others. I'm taking a stand and changing the tradition and the conditioning that was instilled in me. You should too, my beautiful Black Queen! If something is bothering you, speak up. If you're having a bad day, speak up. If you're not feeling 100%, speak up. If you are overwhelmed and need help, speak up. If you want to have a breakdown and cry then cry your eyes out. Superheroes are fictional characters, so why should we model behind something that's not real. That's not realistic. It was made up to give children something to believe in.

What we, as strong Black women, go through daily is not realistic and now it's time to keep it real. It's time to take a stand and normalize for Black women to have emotions, to have our weak moments, to know it's ok to seek help, to seek therapy, and to seek guidance. I want you to know there were many times I told a bald-faced lie thinking, "If I tell them I'm not feeling ok, I may seem weak. If I ask for help, that means I'm not cut out for this." There were many times I would cry alone in the dark having multiple meltdowns because I felt so overwhelmed. There were many times I just wanted to throw in the towel because I felt all alone. There were many times I would step out into the world with my artificial superhero mask and uniform on. I was made up and dressed up with a huge smile on my face. The whispers I would hear… "My God, she is so strong! I wish I was strong like her! Nothing defeats her! She can fix everything!" Truth be told, Black Queen, it's time to reveal who you really are because you have a voice. I understand this can seem intimidating, so I'll go first.

If I could tell the world something, I would say live life and love yourself to the fullest. Life is too short to be miserable, so why sit around and be negative, bringing people down and making their lives hell because you decided that you want to be ungrateful about every single thing. Not me, no, not at all! I love life and I love me! I'm beautiful inside out. When I walk into a room, it lights up as if someone opened the shades and allowed the sunbeams to enter. I feel amazing. I love running my fingers in my tangled tresses and pulling the kinks out to the end, shaking it with that long hair don't care attitude. My smile is bright and contagious. When I smile at you, it makes you want to smile back as though I have you under my spell. This is the day the Lord has made and I'm going to make the most out of it! I enjoy quiet moments sitting by myself, just me and my thoughts. I enjoy listening to old-school hits from 70s R&B to 90s hip hop. I'm content sitting on my sofa bundled up nice and cozy, sipping on some coffee the same color as my skin.

Ahhh… how sweet it is to listen to a hard rain with thunderstorms and lightning in the background. I love the rain! I enjoy cold days outside while in my warm house looking at a good movie with my significant other while the snow comes down causing five inches or more on the ground. When it's all done, you open the door and see the beauty of the snow. There staring you smack in the face… peace! Everything is so still and quiet. These are some of the little things I enjoy, the little things that God gives us. Who would have thought a simple snowstorm could bring on such stillness and peacefulness? Who would have thought?

What's more precious than money? Peace and time. Those two things can bring me the most joy. However, having money can also provide those two things or can it? I had to learn throughout life that time and peace were the two most precious gifts God could ever give me. When I have those two things together I'm at my happiest. Other things make me happy but I can't explain the feeling and joy that I experience when I have the peace and time together. I feel like I'm in another galaxy. I'm in my own peaceful thoughts and the time has stood still for me to enjoy that precious moment. If everyone found that they would be in a better headspace. Their lives wouldn't be so miserable and they would be able to spread that same joy to another person.

These are true words and random thoughts from a strong Black Queen to another. If you were to take the time and have that moment to yourself you would know the things that make you happy and that's what truly makes you strong, my Queen. They are the little things in life that are precious and dear to you. I know you're tired and I hear your cry for help. That's why I wrote you this letter. I thought you should know...

Well, I know you're busy and I have taken up much of your time. I just wanted to write this letter because I thought you should know that it's ok to not be ok. It's ok to be unapologetic. It's ok to protect your peace and time because those are precious. Understand that when that time is gone, you can never get it back. It's ok to ask for help. From one Black Queen to another, I got your back, my sister. You're so precious and strong just like a flawless diamond. A diamond is strong from pressure but is a precious gem. Always remember that just because you're strong doesn't mean you're not a precious gem. Take care of yourself and allow others to as well.

Yours Truly,

Black Queen

Dezire Moore is an introvert with an extrovert wild imagination. A collector of over 100 notebooks and 37 ink pens, Dezire was born with a pen in her hand and stories in her head. She is the author of the *Generational Curse Series: Seductress of the Streets*, which is available on Amazon. Writing has helped Dezire gain the confidence to communicate with the public without any limitations.

I Thought You Should Know

Chapter 11

You Will Hit Rock Bottom

Nicho Charisse

I am sure you have read the title and assumed this letter is for addicts. I ask that you continue to read because this letter is for anyone.

Rock bottom is defined as a time or an event in life that causes an addict to reach the lowest point in their disease. In this letter, I will define rock bottom as a time or an event in a person's life that causes them to reach the lowest point in their lives. The phrase that is commonly used is "sick and tired of being sick and tired".

As you go through life, there are going to be times when you are going to be at your wit's end. What are you going to do about it? When are you going to stop complaining? When do the tears stop falling?

There may be a day that you will be at your job and then suddenly someone who has been there ten or twenty years throws their hands up and walks out. You may discover an employee abandoned their job. They may have no plans, they do not have another job waiting for them and have bills lined up. So, what happened? Did they get tired of watching people who do nothing get promoted? Did someone from the outside get hired in a leadership position that they applied for and must train them? When you are tired of being overlooked, you have hit Rock Bottom. You wake up and before you get out of bed, you may turn off the alarm, pull the covers over your head and say, "I just cannot do this another day". It is time to go. However, why wait until then? There are going to be enough signs for you to begin the process moving on. Research other companies, consider taking a class or two, or if you can, go to college or consider a trade. Do not use the excuse of the number of years (seniority) or because it is close to home. If you do not do anything about your Rock Bottom, your employer will. If you have been thinking about changing careers or starting a business, what is stopping you? The more it tugs at your heart, the more sleepless nights you have because you have so many ideas and your job ignores you, or being tired of living check to check, the more you may become depressed, angry, or stressed. You are hitting your Rock Bottom.

The toxic behavior of relatives and those who make excuses for them will cause a lot of tension. They will try to make you out to be the bad guy because you will not play along. Family can be just as toxic as any other relationship. For example, some relatives feel just because you are considered the successful one of the family that you are supposed to take care of them. I'm not saying there is a problem with helping or assisting, but they must hold up their end of the bargain and show they are trying. There are also relatives who do not encourage and always have something negative to say about everyone, yet they are doing nothing with their lives. There is the relative who knows secrets that can be imperative to your life, have stolen from you and you can hear and see the jealousy. It hurts when it is family, but they are human and have their reasons. These are Rock Bottom moments as well. You will always love your family but some you must love from afar. Do not be guilty. Addicts must walk away from people and situations for them to become clean and sober. Sometimes, you must do the same to cleanse your soul and have a peace of mind. People have had to walk away from their children, as well.

Be advised, friendships are no different. Friends like to guilt trip you. They tend to use the number of years that you have known each other or throw the word loyalty around.

Loyalty is defined as a strong feeling of support or allegiance. Your childhood friend, that BFF that saved you one time 30 years ago and that friend that stuck by you "when no one else would" will use loyalty to cling on to you because of their own flaws. These people may put you into dangerous situations. Every time they are involved in a bad situation (that may be their fault), they call you, you cover for them, you are their financial supporter, and the list can go on and on. No matter how much this is draining your pockets and your spirit, you continue the friendship because of loyalty. Is that really friendship? Is this your rock bottom? What are you going to do about it? As you get older, paths with friends change. You can end friendships. You can have new friends. True friends understand. They are not jealous. Friends want the best for you even if it is not them.

It takes Rock Bottom for couples to find out how strong their relationship are and who is willing to work for it. It can happen at any time and many times within a relationship. When does the abuse end? Will it ever end? Abuse is not always physical. Words hurt just as bad. Often, couples just grow apart, or life takes over and the feelings are just not the same. The older the relationship, the more changes will come. Either one or both people get to the point in which they no longer want the relationship anymore. This is your rock bottom. So, now what? Do you throw it all away or do you try to work it out? Obstacles are a part of life, but it is how you handle those obstacles that creates the happy endings. Before you throw your hands up in disgust and walk away think to yourself, "Is it really worth it?" Just like addicts have sponsors when they feel trouble within them are brewing (the cravings) or just to keep them updated on their progress, couples need help with their rock bottom as well. Counseling or spiritual guidance is one way. Addicts may go to support meetings, couples can go to couples counseling, group meetings and link with other couples. It is something to consider before throwing in the towel. When you get through this, you will be a blessing to someone else. Right now, neither one of you have the guidance to get you through this. But once you get the tools and the knowledge, that's when you share your trials and tribulations, and it is one heck of a story. That is how you grow and begin the healing. Keep in mind, if you are not growing as an individual, you will not grow as a couple. The story may not end how you want it to, but it will be the right ending for you. Finally, you will handle your rock bottom.

Friends, families, and jobs come, go, and change just like the seasons. If they are not fitting in your life during that time, you have hit your rock bottom and it is time to let go. The thing about hitting rock bottom and doing something about, is that you may help the next person deal with their rock bottom. Be an example. You never know who may be watching.

Nicho Charisse is a resident of Pittsburgh, Pennsylvania. This is her fourth collaboration book. Her writings have also appeared in *Reflections on Purpose*; *Dear Depression*; and *In the Morning*. Nicho enjoys creating worlds through her writing and helping people escape their realities.

I Thought You Should Know

Chapter 12

My Socio-Cultural Environmental Relationship Theory

Ellen D. Brown

What causes one person to be faithful in relationships and another person to be unfaithful? Can the reason be biologically based? Is it possible to pass on an "unfaithful" gene to one's offspring, from one generation to the next? Or are there social, environmental, cultural and spiritual factors that influence certain behaviors? How does a person know how to form lasting relationships or how to recognize a bad relationship or how to end a bad relationship and start anew? What guides one in forming relationships? And are there differences or similarities in the way males form relationships and the way females form relationships? My Socio-Cultural Environmental Relationship Theory (SCER Paradigm) examines relationship factors and how they influence relationships and impact the choices one makes in the selection of a mate. This theory I so named because it incorporates several theoretical views regarding the development of personality and the subsequent behaviors. This theory looks at the many factors that impact and influence human behaviors in relationships by attempting to identify the social, cultural, spiritual, environmental and biological factors to better understand how personality traits originate. Here is my theory…

There are different theoretical assumptions regarding how one acquires personality traits and certain behaviors. Some theorists believe that genes play a major role in personality development, while others dispute the biological aspects of personality. I agree with biologically-based gender differences but reject the premise that instincts constitute the driving force in personality. I prefer to side with those theorists who believe that personality traits and behaviors are learned. However, it is undeniable that some differences in males and females are due to genetic make-up. Babies are born male and female. Their brains develop differently and at different rates. Males and females are socialized differently and we respond to boys and girls differently. Our expectations of them are different. Behaviors that are tolerated from one sex may be less acceptable from the other sex. For example, it is acceptable for girls to cry but unacceptable for boys. We have all heard, "Boys don't cry". Boys and men in our society are seen as aggressive, independent and objective. Girls and women are more submissive, dependent and subjective. Our society acknowledges gender differences in the media, in films, in books and in many other ways. A familiar book by John Gray, Men are from Mars, Women are Venus, looks at gender differences. There are gender differences in values, stresses, motivation, intimacy, emotions, conflict management, feelings, showing appreciation, and support systems, the list could go on and on. Men do not have the same needs and capacity for relationship building as do women and men tend to take their cue from other men, particularly other men who share the same culture. There is no unequivocal theory that can be applied to or account for all human behaviors, for acquisition of personality traits, for individual actions and reactions to different situations. It is my contention that preconceptions, race, past experiences, culture and environment play major roles in the development of personality. That they are the building blocks of personality.

The first relationship factor to be considered is sexual identity and will consider how the developments of one's sexual identity affect behaviors. Does the development of sexual identity differ for males and females? What impact does the development of sexual identity have on personality traits? Which behaviors will manifest themselves in adulthood experiences?

Psychologists agree that the development of sexual identity is a major task for both sexes and this task, according to a psychologist, is more difficult for males than females. Psychologists generally agree that autonomy and independence come more easily to boys than to girls and that boys are less interested in relationships and more interested in objects and exploration than girls. Male separate from their mothers pretty easily and find male identity in their fathers or another male figure, if the father is not in the child's life. For females, it is often the mother who is identified with. Females see in their mothers the meaning of womanhood and understand that this is the basic to their identity. Females have an adult woman close to model the meaning of womanhood for them. Fathers also play a part in the forming of their daughter's sexual identity. Through the love and support, a good father enhances the sexual identity of his own daughters. Girls raised without fathers tend to be less sure of their lovability and femininity. They are more vulnerable to depression and promiscuity. Some of these females spend their entire lives looking for "the" man, the man of their dreams, the man who will rescue them, love them, and support them. That man would be the one person they believe they are destined to have, that will fill every need, make them complete and make them eternally happy. This female often goes from one disastrous affair to another, seemingly propelled by sexual motivators. Or are they unconsciously looking for the father that was absent from her life? These females who suffer from "Mother Influence Syndrome" consciously or unconsciously distancing themselves from males that their mother might approve of. This development aspect of growth will play a role in the kind of adult that children will grow up to be. It will impact decision making factors when selecting a mate or when forming relationships. The development of sexual identity, childhood experiences and one's social environment and cultures also contribute to the development of personality traits.

Another relationship factor refers to aspects of childhood experiences... one's social environmental and one's cultures may be factors that contribute to personality traits and behaviors.

We have seen how the development of one's sexual identity may affect personality. Now, let's look at the possible impacts of child rearing. The atmosphere in the home, whether comfortable and loving, or stressful and uncaring, will impact behaviors. Child who grow up in a warm, loving, supportive home and receives encouragement and praise, will know how to love other because they have received love. It is in childhood that we are taught to respect others, we learn manners, to be polite, to compromise, and unwritten laws or rules regarding behaviors. Case in point, as a child, I was taught that one must exhibit certain behaviors to be considered a "lady". For instance, a "lady" never ventures out at night without a male escort and a "lady" never stays out all night. These teachings are still a viable part of my life. We can see that this behavior is learned and remains consistent throughout life. Our society and its double standards impact relationships and create male and female differences as well... relationship factor... societal factors.

Persons are affected by how they will be perceived by others, family, relatives, peers, and friends and will the "acceptable" image necessary for a particular situation. For instance, our society had produced a "macho man". This is the male who has to be tough, to show "his boys" that he is a lover, a "real man" with a lot of "honeys". The macho man does not care much for others. He devotes his energy to his own well-being. He looks out for himself. He is number one. He treats women as sex partners, view marriage as something to be avoided or as a temporary arrangement to be maintained until something or someone better comes along. The macho man would surely be viewed in a negative manner by most females in our society. However, negative actions or behaviors can, and sometimes are, viewed in a positive manner. For instance, males are socialized in a manner that encourages multiple sex partners. This action is viewed positively by other males, "it's a man's thing", while girls, on the other hand, are taught to be respectful and to "act like a lady" and to refrain from sexual activity until she is married. Young men will have sex with a young lady he has little or no regard for and he is taught by other males that he can have all the "play" he can handle as long as he avoids saying, "I love you". Young men are taught to avoid emotional attachments and to move on to the next female. Males are encouraged to engage in sexual activities with females, yet they are warned not to ever take that type of females home to meet their mother and warned to never consider her for a wife. Most young males and females mimic the behaviors of those around them and are the product of what they have been taught regarding acceptable behaviors.

This brings me to another relationship factor... religion and how it impacts behaviors. I believe all people are born good. I also believe that individuals exercise free will in making choices in life. Christian belief impact behaviors and can provide a guide for life choices, for determining what is right or wrong for knowing what is moral and what is immoral. Christianity comes with rewards. That is, if one lives a righteous life, free of sin, he/she will "go to heaven" when he/she dies and have everlasting happiness and joy. On the other hand, if one lives "in sin", he/she dies will go to the fiery flames of hell. For example, a couple who follows religious practices in a relationship and who is considering marriage will receive premarital counseling and practice abstinence. After marriage, this couple will refer to the Bible as a guide to help them sustain their marriage and will abide by the marriage laws of the Bible and refrain from negative behavior, such as adultery. These and other Christian teachings remain consistent through one's life. One's behaviors, whether consciously or unconsciously, will reflect their religious beliefs throughout one's life.

In the home that I grew up in, one was God-loving and God-fearing. There were and still are certain teachings, subconscious, that effect certain behaviors today. For example, these teachings will apply something as basic as saying grace before eating a meal or prying at the beginning and end of each day. These simple behaviors have become a part of who I am and is reflected in all aspects of my life.

Now, some environmental and cultural relationship factors...

There are many idiosyncrasies in determining what is important when forming relationships and there are just as many reasons for choosing to form relationships as there are reasons for opting not to form relationships. For instance, there are specific things that one desires in a mate, such as complexion and hair length and texture. Some males may choose a mate based on size of her hips or size of her breasts. Some women will only date men that are tall, or that have broad shoulders. Both genders tend to select a mate based on how that choice of mate will be perceived by the sufficient others in their lives. I can recall the reaction from my older female family members when I chose to date a dark-skinned man and had the nerve to bring him to a family gathering. Most of my female relatives are color struck and regard dark skin as a negative attribute. Ironically, a large number of relatives have dark complexions.

There are similar unwritten cultural rules that play at part in how one determines what attributes to look for in an acceptable mate. For example, when I was young, it was taboo to date outside one's race. For African Americans to date outside their race was considered a crime in the inner city of Baltimore. A Black brother would not even dream of bringing a female from another race into the hood. His actions would be regarded negatively by others in the neighborhood, including his family members, peers, his "boys" and his other friends. It should be noted that this unwritten rule applied to both genders. There is now widespread and "acceptable" race mixing in Baltimore, in my family and around the world. Those family members in mixed marriages know which family members to avoid socially. They know which members of the family are accepting of the union and can be included in social events. It should be easy to see how one's culture can play a role in the development of certain behaviors, that the behavior was learned and that the behaviors remain consistent over time and situations.

It is plain to see that gender difference exist between males and females. From the time they are born, little girls are much more responsive to people than little boys. Some theorists contend that gender differences are due in part to the differences in brain side and to the differences in the mental capacity of males and females. Little girls smile sooner than boys. Girls are more likely than boys to be emotionally sensitive. Females have a greater need for security and protection and take more responsibility for the wellbeing of those around her, in her mate, her children, her family, relatives and friends. Men are less focused on keeping things in order. Men value status and independence and worry about losing value or status in the eyes of others. They (men) don't want to be outdone by others, tend to be more competitive than women and view problems as a sign of weakness that threaten status. Some of these traits can be attributed to genes, however, some of these traits are learned and behaviors are controlled by conscious or unconscious mechanism.

A person isn't born good or bad. It is through development that a person acquires different personality traits. There are many theories of personality development, each with its own premise as to what impacts/influences personality traits and subsequent behaviors. These traits are influenced by one's culture, spirituality and by one's social environment. Society has defined what acceptable behavior is, and people modify behavior by rational thought and cultural influence. Spirituality can further influence behavior by giving people a sense of right and wrong. People are motivated by rewards and punishment, the tendency to seek pleasure and avoid pain. They are unconscious mechanisms to keep anxiety-provoking thoughts in the unconscious mind and out of awareness and consciously prevent negative behaviors from actions manifesting. People have the ability to choose course of action. Most humans, children and adults, seek those things in life that brings pleasure and avoids those things or situations in life that knowingly create discomfort, unease or pain. However, there are sometimes negative aspects of children's development that has lifelong consequences. Children that are brought up in loving, supportive, spiritual home will become loving adults with goals and a positive view of life and they will feel good about themselves. If, on the other hand, a child is reared in a home with no love and support, that may have been abused or neglected, then he/she may become an unhappy, unloving adult without future goals or aspirations. An example would be the individual that has been sexually abused as a child. He/she may grow up with a dependency on sexuality as a means to feel wanted or loved. They may indulge in unhealthy sexual practices and may have problems establishing relationships.

A fully functioning person, is one that can express intuition and emotion, has a desire to build great relationships, has a feeling of belonging, is loved and knows how to love. A person who can recognize problems in life and in relationships and are able to find solutions. This person has established a sense of balance and feels comfortable with the decisions that they have made in life. They are at peace with themselves and they have a spiritual foundation that can give them strength and hope for the future, the guidelines for a happy, productive life. Everyone feels the physical and mental strains of stress at some point in their lives. Life stresses are a natural part of life and it is how one handles these stresses, disappointments, and obstacles that determine the quality of life for the individual. A person who feels lost, depressed or insecure, may have low self-esteem and may conceal their true identity to protect themselves. These individuals may allow these stresses to lead to detrimental coping methods, such as excessive eating or alcohol and/or drug use.

Finally, I believe that one can overcome negative childhood experiences by cultivating a positive image of him/herself and by working toward achieving goals in life. If you don't know your own goals, you can't effectively match yourself with a mate. What's most important to the success of any relationship is a mutual desire on the part of each person to a "true" relationship, based on honesty and integrity. Both must be committed to the idea of a participatory relationship with give and take. Both must share the same values, structure and goals in the relationship. Once can have a healthy life if one has strong confidence in themselves, has positive resolution to problems and controls and controls one negative behaviors. Lastly, and most importantly, a healthy relationship will flourish and one can have a happy, prosperous life through understanding that there is a divine order, that God has a plan for one's life and that relationship building is a day-to-day process.

Ellen D. Brown is a Baltimore native, mother of two grown sons, two grown grandchildren, and three great grandchildren. This writing was extracted from a 2004 class assignment in social work. In her spare time, Ellen enjoys reading, writing, and watching television and movies.

I Thought You Should Know

Chapter 13

A Weekend on the Block

Beatrice M. Hunter

If you are Black and was coming of age during the turbulence of the 1960s, I venture to say you had a Fifth Street in your town. Fifth Street was the black business and social hub for black people in just about every city or town during the years of segregation. It was where you went to meet and greet your friends, where your needs for recognition as a person was met. Fifth Street supplied your family needs, where black grocers issued you credit, knew your name, and the names of your family. Your doctors' offices, dentists, insurance companies, and even a black lawyer or two had their offices on Fifth Street. It was a place where you rose above the pressures of the dying vestiges of segregation and breathed in the air of equality and freedom.

During the 70s, it was the stage we walked across from childhood into adulthood and declared our independence from the prohibitions of our parents in the years before. We strutted up and down the streets of "The Block" from Madison Street (where not much was happening) for five blocks to Taylor. We were debuting our independence on the famous or infamous stage of Fifth Street.

Speaking of stages...our most prized stage was the "Club". Its real name in my town was the "Sportsman Club". We knew nothing of its history of being built by a freedman of color to serve as a professional building for black professionals who had nowhere else to serve their community. And at 18, we didn't care. What we cared about was getting in the joint. The Club was now where local youth bands exhibited their talents, from young high schoolers such as Fats and the Continentals to the older bands such as the Jivers. The Club also hosted famous entertainers such as James Brown, Jackie Wilson, and Roy C. It was the place to be. But after their shows, many had no place to stay because hotels wouldn't let them stay in their establishments. Someone came up with the idea of a traveler's book for black folks, informing them of places safe to stop for gas and spend the night... the Green Book.

Many times, in towns such as mine, Blacks who brought the singers to town would have to put them up. Yes, Fifth Street was the place to be. On Fridays, men rushed home from the foundries and factories, dressed to impress, splattered Old Spice all over, untied the "Conk" and dipped to Fifth Street after a week of bowing and work fit more for a mule than a human. For us, our Fridays found many of us getting our hair done in the latest styles in some neighbor or another's kitchen. There were plenty of burnt ears on Fridays from the hot combs in practically every house. Dresses far too short were pulled from hidden spaces in the closets, bright red lipstick matured our lips, Avon cologne insured we smelled loud and enticing if we were lucky enough to get a slow drag. By this time, many girls no longer stuffed their bras to look old enough for admission, as many of us had done in the past when we neither could afford nor were the right age to get in. In years past, most of us had to be satisfied listening from our windows to the music from whatever group employed that night. The sound permeated all the streets bordering Fifth, which was so long. But this time was different. We were getting ready to go to *the* Club!! We were old enough and no one could tell us no.

The doors opened around 9 p.m., but no one wanted to be among the first there; we had to make a grand entrance. So, it was usually 10 p.m. before we ascended the stairs. After finally getting to the dance floor, we stood there in the shadows letting our eyes adjust to the dimness before darting around to see who we knew who was there, what they were wearing, and who they were with.

Saturdays and Sundays were just as crowded. The weekends on Fifth gave us the opportunity to meet and greet our neighbors, enjoy some good music, and throw off the shackles of long work weeks. Today, the Fifth Street we knew has been abandoned and demolished, a form of genocide. Also gone is the importance it once played in the African American community during segregation when it was solely black owned and utilized. Fifth Street of yesterday no longer grew; it was no more "Chicken Soup for the Black Soul".

Businesses closed, the Sportsman was knocked down to make way for a parking lot, and the youth that once made it a second home went inside for good. The mecca of the Black community was seemingly dying right before our eyes. So, although the Fifth Street of my youth is no more, as I imagine yours is also only a memory, I shall forever carry the lessons and memories into my senior years. Fifth Street had a soul, the soul of visiting dignitaries, entertainers, civic and social leaders, ministers, and entrepreneurs of its heyday. Sit and watch the changes. If you know Fifth like we knew Fifth, walk the "Block" and feel for yourself the rhythms and heartbeat of a glorious and struggling past. I'm so glad we had a Fifth Street.

Beatrice M. Hunter is a mother of an African American King, and Queen, a grandmother of noble nine, and great grandmother of five royals. Her family's nobility was not granted by man, but by being born African American and the higher power of us all. Her desire is to leave a legacy for her offspring and those to come through genealogical research.

Beatrice's passion is researching local history and imparting whatever lessons she has learned to the youth of today. She has been blessed to have various articles published in local venues, give talking sessions to college students, and is currently writing two book.

I Thought You Should Know